Dear Parent:

Congratulations! Your child is taking a powerful step on an exciting journey with God and His word.

This book will help your child create the future God desires for them by building a strong relationship with Him. It does this by teaching them to speak the promises of God over themselves.

Your child will have the scriptures of God's word right at hand when they read this book. The impact on

Future generations from children reading this book will be amazing!

So parents, can I count on you to make sure your child has this book in their hands, and that they are reading it? I believe this book will also impact the parents as their children are reading it..

HAVE YOUR KIDS SPEAK THE WORDS OUT LOUD WITH PASSION!!

Proverbs 18:21 says life and death, are in the power of the tongue.

Someone at school told Mary she wasn't beautiful.

Manny says, "Speak it Kiddo!"

"God you said, I am your masterpiece.
I am your incredible work of art,
and you love me greatly".
(Ephesians 2:10)

Manny's dog ran away from home,
and it caused Manny to be very sad.

Mary says, "Speak It Kiddo!"

"God you said,
you will give me beauty for ashes."
(Isaiah 61:3)

Mary is afraid to climb the tree,
to get into the club house.

Manny says, "Speak it Kiddo!"

"God you said I can do all things
through Christ who strengthens me."
(Philippians 4:13)

Manny and Mary are praying together in their room before bedtime.

Manny and Mary say, "Speak it Kiddo!"

"God you said when two or three are gathered, you are in the midst.
God we thank you that our family is blessed, prosperous, and healthy. In Jesus' name, Amen!"
(Matthew 18:20)

Manny is running for president of his class,
but Manny doesn't think he can win the election.

Mary says, "Speak it Kiddo!"

"God you said, I am confident and fearless,
and you always cause me to triumph in Christ Jesus."
(2 Corinthians 2:14)

Mary is trying out for the cheerleading team, but she doesn't think she has the skills to make the team.

Manny says, "Speak it Kiddo!"

"God you said I will flourish like a palm tree."
(Psalm 92:12)

Mary and Manny are last in line
to get on the roller coaster.

Manny and Mary say, "Speak it Kiddo!"

"God you said I am the head and not the tail.
In Jesus' name, Amen."
(Deuteronomy 28:13)

Manny and Mary see a lonely boy at school.
They go and make friends with him.

Manny and Mary say, "Speak it Kiddo!"

"God you said to love others as I love myself."
(Mark 12:31)

Manny was told that he wasn't good enough
to make the basketball team.

Mary says, "Speak it Kiddo!"

"God you said I am anointed, accepted,
and approved."
(1 John 2:27, Galatians 1:10, Romans 14:18)

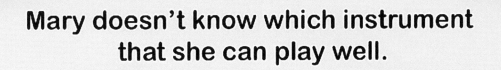

Mary doesn't know which instrument that she can play well.

Manny says, "Speak it Kiddo!"

"God you said that everything my hands touch will prosper."
(Deuteronomy 30:9)

Manny and Mary say, "Speak it Kiddo!"

"God you said honor my father and mother,
so that we will live a long time
in the land God is giving us."
(Exodus 20:12)

Manny is very afraid to walk to school by himself.

Mary says, "Speak it Kiddo!"

"God you said,
you order your angels to protect me wherever I go."
(Psalm 91:11)

Mary isn't feeling well.

Manny says, "Speak it Kiddo!"

"God you said by Jesus' stripes, we are healed."
(Isaiah 53:5)

Manny has to play soccer against
a kid that looks like a giant.

Mary says, "Speak it Kiddo!"

"God you said I will never be shaken."
(Psalm 112:6)

Mary and Manny are out of lemons
at their lemonade stand.

Manny and Mary say, "Speak it Kiddo!"

"God you said you shall supply all of our needs
according to your riches in Christ Jesus."
(Philippians 4:19)

Mary is afraid of the dark.

Manny says, "Speak it Kiddo!"

"God you said you are always with me.
I trust you to protect and comfort me."
(Psalm 73:23)

Manny encourages Mary to ride her new bike.

Manny says, "Speak it Kiddo!"

"God you said as iron sharpens iron,
so another sharpens another."
(Proverbs 27:17)

Manny and Mary prayed that their family would move
into a big beautiful home.

Mary and Manny say, "Speak it Kiddo!"

"God you said you would bless us
more than we can imagine."
(Ephesians 3:20)

Manny and Mary are happy and grateful
that God is blessing them.

Manny and Mary say, "Speak it Kiddo!"

"God you said praise proceeds the victory,
so we thank you."
(1 Peter 2:9)

Manny and Mary feel the love of God surrounding them.

Manny and Mary say, "Speak it Kiddo!"

"God you said you love us with unfailing love."
(Psalm 117:2)

Mary is having a race against girls that look stronger and faster than her.

Manny says, "Speak it Kiddo!"

"God you said if I have faith the size of a mustard seed, I can move mountains."
(Matthew 17:20)

Manny made a bad grade on his test in school.

Mary says, "Speak it Kiddo!"

"God you said you have plans to prosper me
and not to harm me."
(Jeremiah 29:11)

Mary and Manny love to read their bibles
first thing in the morning.

Manny and Mary say, "Speak It Kiddo!"

"God you said put your kingdom first,
and do what you want us to do,
then all of those things will also be given to us."
(Matthew 6:33)

Manny and Mary give away clothes and shoes
to kids that are less fortunate.

Manny and Mary say, "Speak it Kiddo!"

"God you said give, and a good amount
will be poured into your lap. It will be pressed down,
shaking together and running over.
(Luke 6:38)

Manny and Mary ask their father and mother
to pray for their family.

Manny and Mary say, "Speak it Kiddo!"

"God you said as for me and my house,
we will serve the Lord."
(Joshua 24:15)

Manny and Mary love to be in the house of the Lord.

Manny and Mary say, "Speak it Kiddo!"

"God you said if we are planted
in the house of the Lord we will flourish."
(Psalm 92:13)

Mary knocked her mother's shiny vase off of the table.
Mary thought she would get in big trouble.

Manny say, "Speak it Kiddo!"

"God you said your grace is sufficient for me."
(2 Corinthians 12:9)

Manny and Mary have to clean up their room
before they can go outside and play.

Manny and Mary say, "Speak it Kiddo!"

"God you said you are the author
and the finisher of our faith."
(Hebrews 12:2)

Manny sees the perfect baseball glove
in a store window that he has dreamed of getting.

Mary says to Manny, "Speak it Kiddo!"

"God you said if I take delight in you,
you will give me the desires of my heart."
(Psalm 37:4)

Mary loves to look in the mirror.

Manny says, "Speak it Kiddo!"

"God you said I am created in your image.
You have placed a hand of blessing on my head,
and you call me blessed."
(Genesis 1:27, Psalm 139:5, Malachi 3:12)

Manny and Mary want you to speak
these words aloud Kiddo!!!!

I AM BLESSED!

I AM PROSPEROUS!

I AM ANOINTED!

I AM FEARFULLY AND WONDERFULLY MADE!

I AM THE HEAD AND NEVER THE TAIL!

I AM STRONG AND MIGHTY IN THE LAND!

I AM A CHILD OF THE HIGHEST GOD!
IN JESUS' NAME, AMEN!

James Williams, debut book Speak It Kiddo, gives us a powerful book of children speaking the promises of God, into real life situations.

Raised in Flint, Michigan, Williams always felt that if he had spoken the promises of God over his childhood, his life would be different. Not knowing his childhood pain would become his purpose. In his debut picture book, James Williams shares with children, when you believe and speak the word of God out of your mouth in any situation, that situation has to change.

Touching and powerful, each page was written by laboring in God's word, through prayer and devotion time to God. This book is both accessible and emotionally charged; each page will have an amazing impact on your child's heart and future. Williams's love for God and children reflects the joy of seeing family generations changed, because of children's hearts being turned towards God at an early age. Despite the fact that he didn't grow up in a home were God's word was continually spoken, his love of God's word came alive on the inside of him, and it inspired him to touch children's lives through this book.

CPSIA information can be obtained at www.ICGtesting.com
Printed in the USA
LVIW01n2142081216
516479LV00003B/11